Health Visitor

Written by Deborah Chancellor
Photography by Chris Fairclough

FRANKLIN WATTS
LONDON•SYDNEY

First published in 2005 by Franklin Watts
96 Leonard Street, London EC2A 4XD

Franklin Watts Australia
45-51 Huntley Street, Alexandria, NSW 2015

© Franklin Watts 2005

Editors: Caryn Jenner, Sarah Ridley
Designer: Jemima Lumley
Art direction: Jonathan Hair
Photography: Chris Fairclough

The publisher wishes to thank Sheena, the staff at Saffron Walden
Community Hospital, the children and staff at St Mary's CE
Primary School, Saffron Walden, and Caitlin, Connie, Emma, Jacob
and Joseph for their assistance with the book.

A CIP catalogue record for this book
is available from the British Library

ISBN 0 7496 6055 4

Dewey decimal classification number: 362.1'4

Printed in China

Contents

I am a health visitor

A health visitor is a special kind of nurse. My name is Sheena.

I work with children and their families. Sometimes, I visit patients in their own homes.

At my office

I have an office at the local hospital. I make phone calls in the office, to arrange my home visits.

I share the office with a team of health visitors.
We have meetings to talk about our work.

A baby clinic

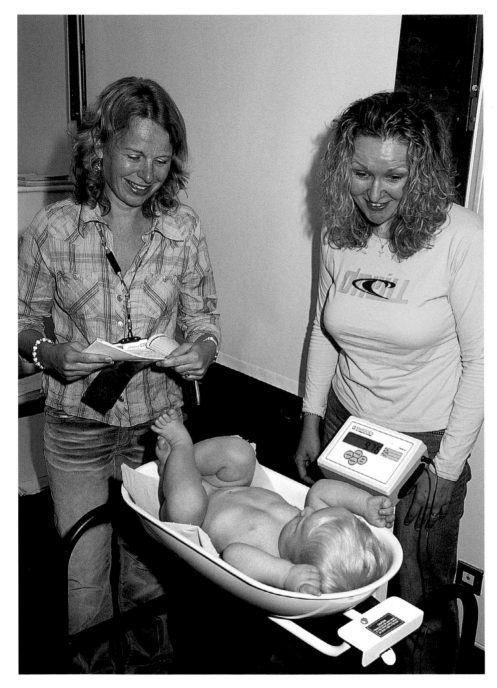

Once a week, there is a baby clinic at the hospital.
I weigh and measure babies, to check they are growing properly.

Small children
have to sit down
to be weighed.
I write down
Caitlin's weight
in her health
record book.

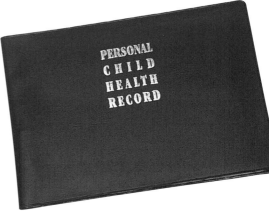

Out and about

When I go on home visits, I take
my equipment with me in my car.

Before I set off, I check the patient's address.
Then I look at my map, to work out how
to get there.

Visiting a newborn

I often visit newborn babies.
Baby Connie is just 13 days old.

I take some measurements, and write them down in Connie's health record book.

A baby health check

I do some special tests with newborn babies. I check that Connie's legs and hips are strong and healthy.

I weigh Connie
on my weighing
scales. She is
feeding and
growing very
well.

A home visit

Children change a lot in the first few years of their lives. I visit children when they are two years old, to see how they are getting on.

Emma and Jacob are twins. They show me how they play. I listen to how they talk.

A child health check

Jacob is very good at standing on one leg. This shows me that he can balance.

I look in Emma's eyes with a small
torch, to check that they are healthy.

A school visit

Sometimes I visit schools to tell
children about my work.

This class is learning about babies.
We talk together about how babies grow and change.

Busy days

The children take turns to weigh
a doll on my weighing scales.

My job is always busy,
but it is great fun.
Every day, I meet and help
lots of different people.

Useful equipment

The health visitor weighs babies on these **weighing scales**.

The health visitor gives parents helpful **information leaflets** about children.

The health visitor uses her **mobile phone** to contact patients when she is out of the office.

The health visitor writes
all her appointments in a
work diary.

The health visitor watches
children play with these **toys**,
to see how they are growing
and changing.

Information about a
child's health is written in a
health record book.

Growing up

When you are born, you cannot sit, crawl or walk. By the time you are one, you can do most of these things – and even begin to talk.

Many more big changes happen soon after this. By the time you start school, you can talk, run, hop and jump!

You need to eat healthy food to help your body grow. Eat lots of different types of fruit and vegetables. Drink plenty of milk and water. Get moving - run around, play and dance to keep fit, and walk to school if you can.

Glossary and index

baby clinic - a place where parents and babies can meet a health visitor. **Page 10**

health check - an appointment to make sure that a patient is well. **Pages 16, 20**

health record book - a book with information about a child's health. **Pages 11, 15, 27**

health visitor - a nurse who sees patients at home, or in a clinic. **Pages 6, 9, 26, 27**

home visit - an appointment at a patient's home. **Pages 8, 12, 18**

newborn - a baby that is only days or a few weeks old. **Pages 14, 16**

weighing scales - equipment to measure a patient's weight. **Pages 17, 24, 26**